Original title:
Echoes of Emotions Unspoken

Author: Thomas Sinclair
ISBN HARDBACK: 978-9916-90-622-4
ISBN PAPERBACK: 978-9916-90-623-1

The Inward Journey of Hidden Truths

In shadows deep, the secrets lie,
A heart that whispers, but cannot cry.
Footsteps echo on forgotten trails,
Where silence weaves its somber tales.

In the mirror of the soul's own gaze,
Resilience shines through the darkest haze.
Veils once thick begin to part,
Revealing light within the heart.

Softest Echoes of the Unsaid

Between breaths, the unspoken lingers,
A gentle touch of unseen fingers.
Words hover like the morning mist,
Promises formed, but never kissed.

In every glance, a universe waits,
Soft truths hide behind the gates.
Echoes of feelings yet to arise,
In silent whispers, love never dies.

The Unfurling of Stifled Words

Like petals pressed in a weathered book,
Stifled words wait, longing to be shook.
With every dawn, a chance to speak,
To let the silence tremble and peek.

Unfolding stories wrapped in fear,
In brave moments, they finally clear.
Voices rise from their muted clay,
Breath becomes a newer day.

Closing Doors of Unexpressed Thought

Behind closed doors, the battles rage,
With thoughts unvoiced, they fill the cage.
A mind on fire with untold dreams,
Caught in webs of silent screams.

Each door that shuts, a chance forsaken,
In echoes of what was not taken.
Yet hope still flickers through the seams,
For every heart holds fractured beams.

Yesterdays Floating on the Wind

Memories drift like leaves in fall,
Whispers of laughter, echoing call.
Fragments of time, soft and light,
Bearing the dreams lost to night.

Shadows of moments, fading away,
Caught in the breeze, they sway and play.
Ghosts of what was, float on high,
Woven in twilight, beneath the sky.

Time like a river, ever flows,
Carving the path where no one knows.
Yet in the silence, they find their place,
Yesterdays linger, a gentle embrace.

The wind carries secrets, old and true,
Tales of the past, known by few.
Each breath of air, a story to tell,
Yesterdays floating, where memories dwell.

Crickets Chirping in the Dark

Under the cloak of the night so deep,
Crickets sing songs while the world's asleep.
Their rhythmic chorus fills the calm,
Nature's heartbeat, a soothing balm.

Moonlight dances on blades of grass,
Casting shadows where whispers pass.
Each chirp a note of a tune so sweet,
A symphony played at the night's heartbeat.

Stars twinkle like diamonds, bright and clear,
Crickets create a song for the ear.
In the stillness, alive they thrive,
Melodies weave every night, they survive.

So listen closely, to the dark's embrace,
In the silence, hear the crickets' grace.
Their serenade, a world of dreams,
Crickets chirping, as night gently gleams.

Flickers in the Fabric of Time

Moments drift like autumn leaves,
Echoes whispering soft pleas.
Time unravels, threads entwined,
In the glow, memories aligned.

Stars blink in the velvet night,
Wishes born in radiant light.
Each heartbeat marks a fleeting grace,
In the dance of time, we find our place.

Silent clocks, they softly chime,
Reminding us of fleeting prime.
Yet in the shadows, dreams ignite,
Flickers found, just out of sight.

In the tapestry of our days,
Moments carved in countless ways.
Each flicker, a thread sublime,
Woven deep in the fabric of time.

Shadows cast by Unfathomed Desires

Whispers ride on the night breeze,
Unfathomed dreams, a heart's unease.
Shadows dance in candlelight,
Echoes haunting, stealing flight.

Longing lingers, a silent call,
Promises made in shadows fall.
Unseen futures weave their fate,
In shadows cast, we hesitate.

Yearning blooms, an aching flame,
Each desire, a whispered name.
In the dark, we search and seek,
For the courage that feels so weak.

Yet in the depths, hope remains,
Through the shadows, love sustains.
In the quiet, truth's sweet fire,
Awakens shadows of desire.

The Unheard Melody of Love

In the stillness, a soft refrain,
A melody, sweet yet feigned.
Love's notes flutter, shy and meek,
In silence, hearts begin to speak.

Gentle breezes carry sighs,
Unheard songs in the moonlit skies.
Notes unplayed, yet deeply felt,
In love's embrace, the world can melt.

Each heartbeat, a drum unknown,
In the vastness, we find our own.
Though silence reigns, it fills the air,
The unheard melody, a tender prayer.

In the quiet, souls align,
Listening close, our hearts entwine.
Through every hush, we rise and soar,
The unheard love, forevermore.

Unwritten Verses in the Air

Words unspoken float above,
In the space where we share love.
Each breath holds a precious line,
In the silence, our hearts combine.

Dreams drift like clouds so light,
Unwritten verses dance in flight.
Thoughts like feathers gently sway,
In the air, our hopes at play.

Moments linger, soft and rare,
In the breeze, our thoughts lay bare.
Each glance a verse, a story rare,
Unwritten poetry fills the air.

Together we weave, hand in hand,
A tale of love, a vast land.
In unwritten verses, we find our way,
In the air, our hearts will stay.

The Unseen Dance of Unexpressed Love

In shadows soft where whispers dwell,
A silent waltz, a tale to tell.
With every glance, a spark ignites,
Yet words remain, elusive sights.

Hearts entwined in secret sway,
Beneath the moon's enchanting ray.
A dance of souls, no need for speech,
In silence, love learns how to reach.

Unfolding dreams in quiet grace,
In hidden corners, we embrace.
The unseen rhythm, soft and pure,
A bond so deep, forever sure.

Tides of Emotion Beyond Words

Waves crash softly on the shore,
Emotions rise, forevermore.
Each whisper of the ocean breeze,
Holds secrets that bring hearts to ease.

In varying depths, our feelings flow,
A current strong, whatever we show.
Words may falter, but tides won't lie,
For love is vast, as the endless sky.

In moonlit nights, our spirits roam,
In waves of trust, we find our home.
Beyond the shores, we seek, we yearn,
For depth of love, our hearts still burn.

Uncharted Waters of the Heart

Sailing forth on seas unknown,
With every breath, our courage grown.
In stormy skies, we chart the stars,
Through tempest winds, we bear our scars.

Each wave a test, each swell a chance,
In unison, we face the dance.
From depths of fear to heights of joy,
Our hearts collide, a love to buoy.

In gentle tides, we find our place,
With every tide, a warm embrace.
Through waters dark and shores of light,
We navigate our souls in flight.

Simmering Feelings Beneath Still Waters

Beneath a calm and mirrored face,
A tempest brews, a hidden space.
The stillness holds a quiet storm,
Where tender sparks take shape and form.

Emotions bubble, softly rise,
A dance of truth behind the guise.
In silence thick, we dare to dream,
With every glance, a silent scream.

As ripples form beneath the skin,
Our hearts collide, our journey begins.
For in the depths, a glow will spark,
And love will light the endless dark.

A Symphony of Unsounded Chords

In shadows deep where echoes dwell,
The silent notes weave tales to tell.
Each breath a whisper, each sigh a sound,
In stillness, music's pulse is found.

Strings of the heart that softly play,
Harmonies lost at end of day.
With every heartbeat, rhythms rise,
The unseen song beneath the skies.

Crescendo builds in quiet air,
Yet none can hear the moments rare.
In solitude, the mind creates,
A symphony that never waits.

So let us dance to tunes unseen,
In dreams where every tone's serene.
For souls entwined in gentle chords,
Compose a world beyond the words.

The Pulse Beneath Quietude

In silent rooms where shadows creep,
The heartbeats echo, soft and deep.
With every tick, a story grows,
In quietude, the stillness flows.

Eyes closed tight, we feel the beat,
The world outside can't touch our heat.
A pulse that whispers in the dark,
Where solitude ignites a spark.

Beneath the calm, a tempest swells,
In hushed tones, the secret dwells.
Moments caught in time's embrace,
A sanctuary, a sacred space.

So listen close when silence reigns,
For in the stillness, life remains.
The pulse beneath the quietude,
A rhythmic dance of solitude.

Clouds of Yearning in the Night Sky

High above, where dreams take flight,
Clouds of yearning paint the night.
Floating softly on starlit streams,
Carrying our whispered dreams.

Each puffy shape, a wish we cast,
In the vast sky, our hopes are amassed.
As moonlight bathes the canvas bright,
We chase our shadows, into the light.

Beneath the veil of endless blue,
A tapestry of thoughts come true.
Clouds of longing drift and glide,
In the night sky, our hearts reside.

So let us wander through the night,
And find our way by starlit light.
For in the clouds, our spirits soar,
In each soft curve, we yearn for more.

Barriers of Unfolding Sentiments

In walls built high, emotions hide,
Each brick a fear we dare not bide.
Yet cracks appear where light can seep,
In broken barriers, secrets keep.

Tender whispers brush the air,
Unfolding feelings, raw and rare.
With every pause, our breaths align,
Unraveled thoughts that intertwine.

We weave our words with threads of grace,
And break the silence, heart to face.
The barriers tremble, start to fall,
As love's soft echo breaks the wall.

So let us shed our guarded guise,
And meet each other with open eyes.
For in the spaces where we dare,
Lie sentiments that long to share.

The Secret Garden of Unspoken Affection

In twilight's glow, where shadows blend,
A garden holds the things we mend.
Petals fall without a sound,
Love's whispers lost, yet still profound.

Beneath the leaves, the secrets lie,
In every breeze, a muted sigh.
Among the blooms, our hearts entwined,
In silence shared, true love defined.

The moonlight bathes the earth in dreams,
Where every glance, a quiet gleam.
No words to break the sacred trust,
In this stillness, hope is a must.

Time stands still in this enchanted place,
Each fleeting touch, a soft embrace.
Through tender silence, love will grow,
In the secret garden, hearts will know.

Where Silence Whispers

In the stillness of the night,
Where shadows dance in silver light,
Silent stories drift and weave,
In hush, our souls believe.

Each quiet moment, a gentle sigh,
The unspoken words we let fly.
Under stars, our hearts align,
In this void, your hand in mine.

Softly echoes the heart's refrain,
In silence, we find joy and pain.
Every pause, a world to see,
Where close is far, yet we're free.

So let the quiet hold us tight,
In shadows deep, where love ignites.
In whispers soft, our truth revealed,
In silent depths, our fates are sealed.

Veils of Unshed Tears

In the corner of the eye, a glimmer,
A quiet ache, the heart's soft swimmer.
Veils of tears hang, thick and slow,
In silence, sorrows start to grow.

Behind closed doors, the heartache sleeps,
In stillness, the comfort it keeps.
Each drop a tale of joy and woe,
In the hidden depths, our truths flow.

Time may pass, but pain stands still,
In breaking hearts, a quiet thrill.
Yet here we stand, lost in the gray,
Where unshed tears softly play.

But hope still flickers, faint and bright,
In the shadows that hold the night.
For even tears can cleanse and heal,
In their embrace, our souls reveal.

The Art of Not Speaking

In the space between the lines,
Where silence fills, the heart divines.
Words left unsaid, a clever game,
In whispered glances, love's aflame.

The quiet dance of two souls near,
A language born without a fear.
In every heartbeat, a gentle art,
Expressing depth where words depart.

We grasp the hands and hold them tight,
In the heavy hush of soft twilight.
In silence shared, we touch the skies,
Understanding blooms through silent eyes.

Let the world fade, let voices cease,
In this stillness, we find our peace.
For in the art of not speaking,
Lies the essence of hearts seeking.

Vowels of the Unvoiced

In shadows where whispers sigh,
Silence sings a tender tune.
Echoes linger, never dry,
Hidden dreams beneath the moon.

A breathless hush, a fleeting glance,
Unspoken tales in stillness weave.
The heart can dare, the soul can dance,
In spaces where we believe.

Vowels stretched in whispered air,
Lost in time, they drift and float.
Voices fade with utmost care,
Yet in their wake, we find hope.

We meet where silence laughs aloud,
In the gaps of sound, we find.
A world more vibrant than a crowd,
In unvoiced feelings, we're entwined.

The Weight of Unshared Words

Heavy hangs the thought unspoken,
Burdens wrapped in threads of fear.
Words unsaid, like glass unbroken,
Hiding truths we long to clear.

Bridges formed from silent yearning,
Connect the hearts and minds we hold.
Fire fades with lack of burning,
In the shadows, warmth grows cold.

Unshared dreams weigh like a stone,
Crushing hope beneath their might.
In brave silence, we are alone,
The night keeps secrets out of sight.

Releasing thoughts we dare to share,
Lightens the heart, sets us free.
With each word, we show we care,
Unlocking paths for you and me.

Chords of Quiet Longing

Softly strummed, the strings do hum,
A melody of what we seek.
In the stillness, feelings come,
Chords of longing, sweet yet weak.

The night air trembles with desire,
Each note a whisper in our hearts.
Flickering flames, a fragile fire,
A song that never quite departs.

Moments linger, just out of reach,
As echoes dance upon the breeze.
Words unspoken, lessons teach,
In the quiet, we find our ease.

Entwined in sounds, we drift away,
To places only dreams can find.
Chords of longing softly play,
In the silence, love is blind.

Unseen Tears on a Canvas of Feelings

Brushstrokes painted from within,
Colors bleed, emotions flow.
Canvas holds the joy and sin,
A masterpiece of ebb and glow.

Unseen tears mark each line drawn,
Expressions of the heart's design.
Behind each hue, a silent dawn,
A story held in vibrant wine.

Layers deep, the truth unfolds,
Where shadows dance and memories play.
In every stroke, a tale retold,
Unseen tears wash fears away.

The art reveals what words conceal,
A language felt but seldom seen.
In this space, emotions heal,
On the canvas where we've been.

Fractured Dreams in Quiet Moments

In shadows dance the fleeting light,
Whispers whisper through the night.
Fragments of a dream untold,
Yearnings fade, yet visions hold.

A sigh escapes, the world stands still,
A heart's desire, a deepened thrill.
Silent echoes, lost in time,
Painting dreams with subtle rhyme.

The Space Between Words

In murmurs soft, a tale unfolds,
Between the lines, the truth beholds.
A silence speaks, the pauses sigh,
In vacant spaces, feelings lie.

Unspoken thoughts in air reside,
Where shadows linger, hopes abide.
Every glance, a message sent,
In quiet realms, the heart is bent.

Confessions of a Silent Heart

Beneath the calm, a tempest brews,
A heart concealed in fragile hues.
Yet every tear, a lesson learned,
A flickering flame, forever burned.

In stillness grows a vibrant ache,
A fragile peace that shapes the wake.
Confessions whispered to the night,
In silent vows, the soul takes flight.

Distant Chimes of Longing

Across the miles, a yearning calls,
In distant chimes, the evening falls.
A melody drifts on the breeze,
Through rustling leaves, a heart's unease.

Each note a wish, each toll a dream,
In twilight's glow, hopes softly gleam.
As echoes fade, the night grows deep,
In longing's hush, the world will sleep.

Ripples of Silence in the Night

In darkness deep, the whispers fade,
A quiet dream in twilight's shade.
The stars above, they softly sigh,
While time drifts slow, like clouds on high.

Beneath the moon, where secrets dwell,
A haunting peace, a gentle spell.
Each heartbeat echoes, soft and clear,
In ripples deep, we lose our fear.

The night enfolds, a tender veil,
Where silence sings a soothing tale.
With every breath, the world gives way,
To calm reflections, night to day.

In tranquil moments, shadows weave,
The tales of souls who dare believe.
Ripples dance on a still lake's face,
In silence, we find our sacred space.

The Hidden Chorus of Our Hesitation

In paused breaths we linger, unsure,
Each choice a door, each step a lure.
Between the lines, our hearts conversed,
A hidden song, our fears rehearsed.

Beneath the smiles, the stories thrive,
In quiet doubts, our dreams arrive.
With every glance, a word unspoken,
A silent pact, a bond unbroken.

What if the time slips gently by?
What if we fall, or learn to fly?
In hesitation, the echoes ring,
A chorus formed, in waiting, we cling.

Yet in the shadows, courage grows,
The hidden strength nobody knows.
With whispered hopes, we stand awake,
To find the path that we must take.

Whispers in the Silence

In stillness, whispers softly bloom,
A secret song within the room.
Each note a breath, a sigh, a prayer,
In silence deep, we find our share.

The world outside, a distant hum,
Yet here, the heartbeats start to drum.
Within the walls, our fears dissolve,
In whispers low, our souls evolve.

Through every pause, a truth unfolds,
In tender tones, the night still holds.
With eyes that speak, we touch the sky,
And find the words we can't deny.

In gentle echoes, love takes flight,
In whispers shared beneath the night.
We gather hopes like fallen leaves,
In silence sweet, our spirit cleaves.

Shadows of Hidden Feelings

In twilight's glow, emotions loom,
Like shadows cast in a quiet room.
Each glance reveals a truth unshared,
In hidden depths, our hearts are bared.

Behind the smiles, a tempest sways,
Unspoken thoughts in twilight's haze.
The silence grows, a fragile thread,
Where hidden feelings dare to tread.

We walk on paths of soft retreat,
In shadows where our secrets meet.
A gentle touch can spark the fire,
Of whispered dreams, of wild desire.

Yet still we pause, in fear we hide,
The shadows dance, where hope's applied.
In tangled webs, our hearts unfurl,
In hidden feelings, we find our world.

Unbreakable Bonds of Unspoken Desire

In the silence, hearts take flight,
A glimmering spark in the night.
Through gentle glances, feelings grow,
A depth of love we both know.

Whispers hang in the air like dew,
The fragrance of dreams, only for two.
Fingers brush in fleeting grace,
In every moment, a warm embrace.

In unseen threads, we are entwined,
In every heartbeat, love defined.
With eyes that speak what lips won't dare,
Together bound, beyond compare.

Forever close, though words stay shy,
Unbreakable bonds that never die.
In every pause, in every sigh,
The truth of us will always fly.

Threads of Yearning in Quietude

In silence, dreams begin to weave,
Soft whispers borne on a gentle eve.
Every thought, a delicate thread,
Drawing closer where souls have led.

Moonlit nights hold secrets tight,
As shadows dance in soft starlight.
With every breath, a silent plea,
Binding hearts in harmony.

The stillness speaks, a sacred space,
Where every gaze reflects your grace.
In the quiet, love finds its way,
Threads of yearning never sway.

Through uncharted realms, we explore,
In quietude, we crave for more.
Two souls intertwined, never apart,
Crafted together, a work of art.

The Weight of What Remains Unsaid

In the silence, truths take form,
Heavy as the gathering storm.
Words unspoken, a haunting weight,
Resting softly upon our fate.

Each glance a plea, a barrier thin,
A story waiting to begin.
With every breath, we linger near,
As if the words may draw us clear.

The weight of longing, pressing down,
In quiet moments, we almost drown.
Yet in this hush, love still can thrive,
In what's unspoken, we come alive.

Through time and space, emotions build,
In heartbeats shared, a void filled.
With every hesitation, desire grows,
In silence, the deepest passion flows.

Solitude's Tender Resonation

In solitude, voices softly blend,
Echoing whispers that never end.
A tranquil heart finds strength in plight,
In loneliness, the soul takes flight.

Gentle moments shared with the breeze,
Nature's embrace puts the heart at ease.
In silent woods where shadows play,
Solitude sings, keeping fears at bay.

Every thought like a feather drifts,
In the stillness, the spirit lifts.
A symphony of one, sweet and clear,
In quietude, I draw you near.

Embracing the calm, I softly learn,
That solitude's warmth will always burn.
Within its arms, I find my song,
In tender echoes, I still belong.

Ink that Lingers on the Page

In shadows deep, the words reside,
Each chapter holds a tale inside.
Whispers caught in ink and quill,
Moments framed, the heart to thrill.

The paper crinkles, folds with care,
A silent dance of thoughts laid bare.
Each sentence soft, a breath of time,
A symphony in quiet rhyme.

Pages turn with hope anew,
Dreams awakened, visions true.
Ink that flows like gentle streams,
Weaving life into our dreams.

As long as hearts can feel and write,
These words will glow, a guiding light.
So let the ink forever stay,
And linger softly on the page.

The Void that Cradles Emotion

In silence deep, the void does call,
Emotions rise, then softly fall.
A heavy weight, yet light as air,
In this stillness, souls lay bare.

The echoes dance, a haunting tune,
Beneath the stars, beneath the moon.
Unseen threads connect the heart,
In this expanse, we play our part.

Reflection pools in darkened night,
The inner world, both calm and bright.
A canvas blank, a silent scream,
Where every thought can roam and dream.

Yet in this void, we find solace,
With every tear, a fragile promise.
Through every heartbeat, every sigh,
We learn to let the feelings fly.

Breaths Entwined in Stillness

In quiet corners, breaths align,
Two souls as one, a space divine.
The world outside begins to fade,
In sweet embrace, our fears betrayed.

With every pause, a moment shared,
The silence deep, yet none compared.
Within the hush, our hearts collide,
In stillness found, we cannot hide.

Time slows down with gentle grace,
Two beating hearts, a warm embrace.
In whispered tones, we share a glance,
Breaths entwined in this romance.

Together here, we find our way,
In tranquil waves where shadows play.
A sacred bond, so pure, so true,
In stillness held, just me and you.

Soft Footfalls of the Heart

With tender steps, the heart takes flight,
Upon the path of dreams and light.
Each touch a whisper, soft and clear,
In every footfall, love draws near.

Silent echoes linger on,
With each new dawn, a sweeter song.
The rhythm sways like leaves in breeze,
In every moment, love's at ease.

Through meadows wide, across the streams,
We navigate our woven dreams.
In gentle steps, the journey's sweet,
Soft footfalls where our spirits meet.

Though paths may twist and shadows creep,
With every heartbeat, love runs deep.
Together here, we'll find our way,
In soft footfalls, come what may.

From the Depths of the Silent Heart

In shadows deep, where whispers dwell,
A quiet ache, a secret spell.
Each beat unheard, a silent plea,
A world unseen, just you and me.

The heart it aches, but never speaks,
In silence strong, the longing peaks.
A gaze that lingers, words unchimed,
In depths of hope, our fates aligned.

Remnants echo, the past's embrace,
Time drifts softly, a tender grace.
Through veils of night, soft embers glow,
A dance of dreams, forever slow.

Yet in this hush, a longing burns,
For truths untold, the heart still yearns.
From silent depths, our spirits rise,
In love's embrace, our hearts are wise.

The Unfinished Portrait of Emotion

Brushstrokes linger, yet colors fade,
A canvas bare, where thoughts cascade.
Each hue a whisper, a story untold,
In fragments lost, our hearts unfold.

The artist's hand, it trembles slight,
Searching for forms in shadows of light.
An unfinished tale, with passion's spark,
In every corner, an echoing mark.

Love's vivid shades, both bright and dim,
Capture the moments, let voices brim.
Yet every stroke, a tear mislaid,
In the portrait's heart, emotions played.

Though incomplete, it speaks so loud,
A lesson learned, both fierce and proud.
In colors splashed, our truths reside,
In this raw beauty, we confide.

Currents of the Unsaid

Beneath the words we never share,
A river flows, a hidden care.
Its depths conceal what eyes can't see,
The currents shift, they carry me.

In silent nights, where secrets creep,
Thoughts unvoiced, like shadows seep.
A longing glance, a fleeting touch,
In the unspoken, we feel so much.

Tangled dreams in the twilight hour,
Unearth the fears, the silent power.
Each unacknowledged, tender sigh,
In silent realms, our truths reply.

The ebb and flow, the heart's refrain,
In quiet spaces, we feel the pain.
Yet in the hush, love's rhythm beats,
In currents deep, our spirit meets.

Wounds Wrapped in Silence

Behind closed doors, the stories hide,
Wounds wrapped tight, pain inside.
Each scar a reminder, a lesson learned,
In stifled whispers, the heart has burned.

The layers thick, a burdened chest,
In silence, we seek, in quiet, we rest.
Though words escape, the hurt remains,
A silent cry, a heart in chains.

Yet light breaks through, a gentle balm,
In tender moments, we find our calm.
Through silent tears, a path reveals,
In facing wounds, the heart can heal.

So let us speak, let silence cease,
In shared stories, we find our peace.
For wounds wrapped tight can finally breathe,
In open hearts, we find relief.

The Language of Untold Thoughts

In shadows deep where secrets dwell,
A whisper stirs, a silent swell.
Words unspoken, feelings near,
A dance of minds, both warm and clear.

Threads of silence weave the truth,
Echoes lost, reclaim their youth.
Beneath the skin, emotions lie,
Hidden tales that yearn to fly.

Dreams float softly, like a song,
Carrying hopes that feel so strong.
In every glance, a story grows,
The language soft, the heart bestows.

Time may fade, the voice may wane,
Yet in the quiet, thoughts remain.
A tapestry of silent sighs,
In us all, the language lies.

Reverberations of the Heart

In quiet chambers beats a sound,
A rhythm felt, unbound, profound.
Each thump, a pulse, a life expressed,
In shadows cast, the heart is blessed.

Moments linger, echoes shared,
From whispers soft, we have declared.
A love that flares like tender light,
Illuminating darkest night.

The path we walk with dreams in hand,
Each step, a promise, bold, we stand.
Reverberations fill the air,
In every heartbeat, love laid bare.

Through trials faced and laughter's song,
Together we shall carry on.
With every beat, a story spun,
The heart's own rhythm, two as one.

Silenced Serenade

Beneath the stars, a quiet plea,
A song unplayed, yet wild and free.
In every note, a silent cry,
Where dreams once soared now gently lie.

The air is thick with muted grace,
Each breath a sigh, a warm embrace.
Melodies lost in midnight's cloak,
A serenade that softly spoke.

In stillness found, the whispers roam,
Gently weaving into home.
A heart once brave, now hushed within,
Yearning for the joy to begin.

Though silence reigns, hope does abide,
In hidden depths, our souls confide.
With every star that lights the sky,
A sweet serenade shall never die.

Beneath the Surface of Still Waters

Reflecting skies of azure blue,
A tranquil realm, both calm and true.
Beneath the surface, shadows glide,
Stories waiting, deep inside.

Ripples dance on fleeting breeze,
Whispers soft among the trees.
Secrets rest where currents play,
In the silence, dreams convey.

Echoes linger, timeless grace,
In quiet depths, a hidden space.
Nature's hush, a soothing balm,
Waves that beckon, soft and calm.

The world above may rush and spin,
Yet below lies peace within.
Beneath the waters, still we find,
A sanctuary for the mind.

The Overgrown Garden of Thoughts

In the garden where dreams grow,
Whispers of petals float and flow.
Memories tangled, wild and free,
Each bloom a thought, lost at sea.

Sunlight dances on the leaves,
Beckoning secrets that the heart weaves.
Among the thorns, beauty thrives,
A testament to how it survives.

Winding paths through shrouded haze,
Guide the wanderer's heart to gaze.
Each rustling breeze a hidden clue,
In this overgrowth, we find the true.

So wander deep, let silence rest,
In this garden, we are blessed.
For every thought that blooms at night,
Is a beacon guiding us to light.

In the Shadows of What Remains

Echoes linger in dim-lit halls,
Whispering tales where silence calls.
Shadows elongated, softly creep,
Where memories linger, hearts do weep.

Faded photos, a ghostly sight,
Capture moments lost to night.
Footsteps timid on the floor,
Haunted by what came before.

In corners dark, the past resides,
Hidden truths that time divides.
Yet within the gloom, a spark ignites,
Reminding us of forgotten lights.

As shadows dance, they softly weave,
Stories that only the brave believe.
In lingering fears, we find the grace,
To embrace the past, and its embrace.

Twilight Echoes in the Mind

The twilight whispers begin to play,
Painting thoughts as night meets day.
In the stillness, shadows blend,
Creating tales that twist and bend.

Stars flicker like distant dreams,
Illuminating life's quiet schemes.
Each echo a memory softly traced,
In the twilight where time is faced.

A gentle breeze stirs the air,
Carrying wishes dashed with care.
In the twilight's tender embrace,
We seek solace, a sacred space.

As darkness unfolds its velvet sheet,
The echoes waltz on silent feet.
In every pause, we hear the call,
Of twilight's echo, uniting us all.

The Undercurrent of Sighs

Underneath the laughter's guise,
Lurk the soft and hidden sighs.
A current flows, unspoken strife,
Woven through the fabric of life.

In crowded rooms, silence sings,
Of burdens carried, invisible strings.
Each yearning heart, a silent plea,
Lost in the hum of what could be.

Raindrops fall like whispered fears,
Cascading down in ancient cheers.
Yet in the still, we find our way,
Through the undiscussed, come what may.

For every sigh that breaks the night,
Holds a fragment of hidden light.
With every breath, we learn to rise,
Above the depths of quiet sighs.

Lurking in the Hush

In the silence shadows creep,
Whispers linger, secrets keep.
Footsteps dance on quiet ground,
Echoes lost, yet still profound.

Moonlight casts a silver glow,
Fingers trace what we don't know.
Breath held tight in the night's embrace,
Stillness wraps this sacred space.

Hearts beat soft beneath the night,
Yearning for some hidden light.
In the hush, the questions rise,
Lurking dreams beneath the skies.

Time suspends, a fleeting glance,
In the calm, we find our chance.
What was lost may soon be found,
In the whispers that surround.

Murmurs in the Void

In the dark where silence breeds,
Murmurs float like autumn leaves.
Fleeting thoughts drift, then depart,
Echoes of a muted heart.

Beneath the weight of endless night,
Voices hover out of sight.
Secrets shared in hidden tones,
In the void, we find our homes.

Questions linger, quiet calls,
Each one waits, in shadows falls.
Yearning for a flicker bright,
In the void, we seek the light.

Whispers lost but never gone,
In this space, we carry on.
Murmurs wrap us in their fold,
Stories waiting to be told.

Balancing on the Edge of Speech

Words dance lightly on the tongue,
Balancing where truths are sung.
Each syllable a careful step,
In this space, silence is kept.

Thoughts cascade like gentle rain,
Falling softly, mixing pain.
Hesitation in the air,
Daring hearts stripped bare.

Moments stretch, time holds its breath,
On this brink, we flirt with death.
Tension builds, a fragile line,
In the pause, we find divine.

Tread with care on edges fine,
In our voices, hopes align.
Balancing, we yearn to speak,
Finding strength within the weak.

The Mystery Beneath Closed Lips

Softly, secrets rustle low,
Beneath the lips, a world to know.
Puzzles wrapped in quiet grace,
Mystery finds its hidden place.

Eyes that gleam with untold tales,
In the night, where silence pales.
Each glance a hint of what lies deep,
In shadows, thoughts we dare to keep.

Closed lips guard the heart's desire,
Flickers of truth, passion's fire.
Behind the veil, intentions glide,
In the silence, dreams abide.

With every breath, a chance to learn,
In whispered hopes, our spirits yearn.
The mystery swirls, yet we remain,
Searching for what love can gain.

Beneath the Veil of the Mundane

In shadows cast by daily grind,
We seek the magic left behind.
A flicker here, a spark ignites,
Transforming hours into nights.

The cup of tea, the way it steams,
A simple act, yet holds our dreams.
We walk the path, our eyes half-closed,
In every breath, the world exposed.

Routine whispers in muted tones,
But in the heart, the fire groans.
Beneath the veil, we rarely see,
The tales of life, the mystery.

So lift your gaze from what you know,
A hidden garden waits to grow.
Each moment holds a secret thread,
Beneath the mundane, magic spreads.

Resonant Silence in the Room

A quiet pause, the clock ticks slow,
In stillness deep, feelings flow.
An echo stirs within the space,
As breaths align, we find our place.

The whispers of what's left unsaid,
Hang in the air like threads of thread.
A knowing glance, a subtle sigh,
In silence, truths are drawn nigh.

The world outside fades far away,
In resonant calm, we choose to stay.
Every heartbeat lays its claim,
In this hush, we feel the same.

The comfort found in muted hours,
Nurtures thoughts like blooming flowers.
Lost in the peace, the room, our home,
In silence deep, we are not alone.

Never Spoken, Forever Held

Words linger deep within the chest,
A treasure trove, a hidden nest.
They swirl like leaves in autumn's breeze,
Caught in the silence, longing to please.

Unvoiced dreams, they softly cling,
To moments missed, the pain they bring.
Yet in the heart, they pulse and swell,
Stories waiting, never to tell.

A gaze can speak what tongues can't share,
In the longing hearts laid bare.
What's unspoken wears a heavy crown,
Yet still it lifts, it won't back down.

Forever held, these truths reside,
Wrapped in the warmth of time beside.
In every breath, the tension grows,
Never spoken, but everybody knows.

Thoughts Suspended in Midair

Like fragile webs that dance on light,
They float between the day and night.
Ideas pause, a breath away,
Caught in a dream, where shadows play.

Fleeting moments, a thought takes flight,\nDrifting softly
through the twilight.
In limbo, they begin to weave,
Stories of hope and what we believe.

In stillness found, we stop to ponder,
The beauty in the act of wonder.
As if to taste the air we breathe,
And find the peace we all perceive.

Thoughts hovering in the quiet space,
Each one a spark, a gentle grace.
Suspended here, they share our plight,
In the embrace of endless night.

Whispers Beneath the Surface

In the depths where secrets lie,
Soft breaths echo, passing by.
Every wave a hidden plea,
Voices tangled, longing free.

Beneath the calm, the storm resides,
Silent tales the water hides.
Feelings drift, a subtle sway,
Unseen truths, they find their way.

A glimmer sparkles in the dark,
Hints of love, an unspent arc.
Silent moments cloak the sound,
In the quiet, dreams abound.

So listen close, the waves will share,
Whispers of hearts laid bare.
For every swell and gentle part,
Beneath the surface, beats a heart.

Silent Reverberations

In stillness, echoes softly call,
Resonating with the fall.
Each heartbeat, like a distant chime,
Suspended in the quiet time.

All around, the silence sings,
Filling gaps in fragile wings.
A melody of dreams unsaid,
Floating softly, gently spread.

Yet in the hush, a tremor grows,
Unseen paths where wonder flows.
Whispers caught in twilight's beam,
Silent echoes of a dream.

So gather close and feel the weight,
Of words that hide, of fate's own slate.
In reverberations, truths align,
In silent realms, your heart is mine.

Shadows of Unvoiced Feelings

In the twilight, shadows merge,
Lingering on the brink of urge.
Silent glances, fleeting sighs,
Unvoiced feelings fill the skies.

Each moment stretches like a thread,
Woven whispers left unsaid.
In shadows cast, the truth may lie,
Treading softly, hearts comply.

Beneath the weight of starry night,
Unspoken dreams take gentle flight.
With every heartbeat, silently,
The shadows weave our tapestry.

So let us dance in muted grace,
Finding solace in this space.
For in the quiet, love shall bloom,
In shadows, we erase the gloom.

Unsaid Words in the Silence

Between the breaths, the silence hums,
A world of thoughts that softly comes.
With every pause, a story waits,
Unsaid words, the heart's debates.

In quiet corners, echoes play,
Filling gaps of what we say.
Weaving futures, bright and bold,
In the silence, our dreams unfold.

Each glance a promise, still unvoiced,
In stillness, we find our choice.
For time stands still, as moments cling,
In unsaid words, our spirits sing.

So linger longer, hear the call,
In silence, we shall have it all.
Let hearts converse where words can't go,
In unsaid whispers, love will grow.

Heartbeats Between Us

In shadows where our secrets dwell,
Two hearts entwined, a silent spell.
We walk the line of what we feel,
In whispered notes, our truth revealed.

With each breath shared, a gentle spark,
In crowded rooms, we find the dark.
An echo sweet, a longing glance,
In fleeting moments, a hidden dance.

Time slows down when you are near,
A silent song only we hear.
Unspoken words between our sighs,
In heartbeats deep, our love implies.

The world outside fades away,
In the stillness, we choose to stay.
In every beat, a promise made,
Together strong, never to fade.

The Language of Unfelt Touch

Fingers grazed the edge of skin,
A thousand words that lie within.
In shadows cast by candlelight,
We speak in silence, hearts ignite.

The weight of words that go unspoken,
In glances shared, the heart is open.
Like autumn leaves on gentle ground,
In every stillness, love is found.

Every moment holds a trace,
Of all the hopes we dare embrace.
In longing sighs, we find our way,
Through realms of night, we choose to stay.

A brush of lips, a fleeting sigh,
In dreams exchanged, we learn to fly.
In every breath, a promise lingers,
The language soft in tender fingers.

Murmurs in the Midnight Air

Beneath the stars, a secret hum,
In whispered tones, our hearts succumb.
The night enfolds us, soft as silk,
In shadows rich, like warmest milk.

Each breath we share beneath the moon,
A symphony, a lover's tune.
The world outside may fade from view,
In every murmur, love shines through.

Time stands still in this embrace,
Where every sigh ignites a trace.
With every heartbeat, whispers bloom,
In midnight's breath, we find our room.

The night is ours, a canvas wide,
With dreams alight, our hearts collide.
In echoes sweet, we paint the air,
With murmurs soft, a love we share.

The Depth of Unexpressed Longing

In the quiet where secrets hide,
A longing deep, I cannot bide.
The weight of wishes in my chest,
An aching truth, a heart suppressed.

Across the miles, I feel your sigh,
A whispered wish that drifts on by.
In every smile, a fateful chance,
Yet in our eyes, we steal a glance.

With every heartbeat, distance grows,
In silence rich, the longing flows.
A sea of thoughts that words can't speak,
In every moment, love feels weak.

Yet deep within, the fire glows,
In unexpressed, the passion flows.
With every breath, my heart will yearn,
For in this depth, our souls discern.

Fragments of the Unsung Soul

In shadows cast by silent dreams,
Whispers linger, soft and low.
A heart that beats beyond the seams,
Hides stories only few can know.

Echoes wander past the years,
Memories weave a subtle thread.
Beneath the weight of unshed tears,
Unseen paths where the brave have tread.

Lost in thoughts of days gone by,
Fragments scattered on the floor.
The unsung melodies don't die,
They linger, waiting to explore.

Hope navigates the endless dusk,
Each flicker sparks a deep desire.
In broken pieces, find the husk,
Of all that's vibrant, bold, and higher.

Celestial Tides of the Heart

Beneath the stars, the ocean sighs,
A rhythm born of ancient night.
Where dreams collide, and vision flies,
The heart can chase the softest light.

Celestial whispers guide the waves,
Pulling love through the cosmic sea.
In each embrace, the spirit braves,
A bond that stretches endlessly.

Tides that rise and fall like thoughts,
Merging shores of fate and chance.
In every heart, a tale is caught,
A dance of souls in a trance.

As moonlight spills on tranquil sand,
We find our place in the grand scheme.
Together, hand in hand we stand,
Chasing the warmth of our shared dream.

When Words Refuse to Dance

In silence, echoes seem to quake,
The pen, it hesitates to write.
When feelings tremble, hearts can break,
Lost in the shadows, void of light.

Thoughts collide in bubbling still,
Fractured phrases yearn to sigh.
The aching need to speak and thrill,
But locked within, they dare not fly.

A waltz of phrases, dormant dreams,
Each word a prisoner, held at bay.
Yet in the void, a spark redeems,
The power of what's left unsaid.

In every pause, a canvas waits,
To capture shadows cast by doubt.
When words refuse to cross the gates,
The heart still knows what love's about.

Painted Passions in the Mist

With brush in hand, the colors blend,
On canvas, secrets start to bloom.
Each stroke a whisper, passion's trend,
Emerging softly through the gloom.

In twilight hues, emotions sway,
A dance of light with shades of dark.
Like fleeting glimpses of the day,
Art breathes where dreaming leaves its mark.

The mist conceals what hearts reveal,
In every layer, stories form.
A tapestry of love's appeal,
Wrapping the lost in a warm charm.

As visions form and shadows trace,
A world unfolds both rich and bright.
Painted passions embrace the space,
Where dreams and realities unite.

The Unseen Thread of Connection

In silence, we weave our unspoken ties,
A bond that transcends the vastest skies.
Like whispers in shadows, subtly spun,
Two hearts align, though they seem undone.

The distance may stretch, yet we feel it near,
A thread that binds, pulling us clear.
Through laughter and tears, it gently flows,
An invisible force that forever grows.

In moments of doubt, when paths seem astray,
This thread will guide us, lighting the way.
For though we may wander, we seldom roam,
This unseen connector will always lead home.

So cherish the ties that can't be unmade,
For in every heartbeat, our love will cascade.
An echo of souls that the world can't confine,
Together forever, forever entwined.

Unwritten Letters to the Stars

I sit beneath the vast, uncharted sky,
Sending my wishes where dreams learn to fly.
Unwritten letters float in the night,
Each star a promise, a glimmering sight.

To galaxies distant, I pen out my hopes,
Where time has no bounds, and love gently copes.
A quiet confession in the cosmic air,
I whisper my secrets, the universe bare.

With ink made of stardust, I draw constellations,
Mapping my heart through galactic vibrations.
Each twinkling beacon, a word left unspoken,
A testament to dreams forever unbroken.

Though paper may crumble and candles may fade,
These letters will linger, a timeless cascade.
To the stars that listen, I send my embrace,
In the silence of night, I find my place.

Reflections in the Stillness

In still waters, the world finds its peace,
A moment of quiet where thoughts find release.
Ripples of silence dance on the surface,
Reflecting the chaos with tranquil purpose.

Beneath the calm, the depth runs profound,
Echoes of whispers can still be found.
Each wave that recedes carries burdens away,
In the stillness, we learn what words cannot say.

Time pauses gently, allowing us grace,
To look within and to trace our own face.
For in reflection, we see all the parts,
The fractured pieces that make up our hearts.

So cherish the stillness, embrace its sweet song,
In the quiet of moments, we truly belong.
With every soft breath, a new truth is born,
In reflections of stillness, our spirits are worn.

The Gap Between Us

Between us, a space often filled with sighs,
A chasm of longing beneath open skies.
Words left unspoken hang thick in the air,
Yet silence can forge a connection so rare.

With every heartbeat, the distance may wane,
In glances exchanged, we manage the strain.
For love knows no limits, though miles may extend,
In dreams we converge, on each other depend.

Through valleys of doubt, we find our own way,
As time bridges gaps that life tries to sway.
With patience, we learn to embrace the unknown,
The gaps that divide us, in time will be sewn.

In essence, our hearts know the paths we must take,
To bridge all the spaces, together we'll make.
So walk through the distance, let it not confine,
For love finds its way, and stars will align.

Whispers of a Forgotten Dream

In the twilight, shadows play,
Silent echoes drift away.
Memories linger, soft and dim,
Yearning hearts in twilight's brim.

Once bright visions fade to grey,
Softly calling, they delay.
Stars above, a distant spark,
Guiding dreams lost in the dark.

Gentle sighs in evening air,
Traces of a love laid bare.
Whispers haunt the midnight hour,
Fleeting thoughts like wilting flower.

Yet within, the heart retains,
Fragments of those vibrant chains.
Though forgotten, not erased,
In the quiet, hope embraced.

The Quiet Storm within

Beneath the calm, the tempest brews,
Silent thunder, whispers muse.
A heart beats like distant drums,
Restless soul, the quiet hums.

Lightning dances in the mind,
Thoughts collide, both fierce and kind.
A storm rages, yet remains
A secret locked in hidden chains.

Through the calm, the shadows creep,
Silent vows, a promise deep.
In the eye, the stillness reigns,
Yet hope flickers, love sustains.

As clouds gather, fears take flight,
Finding solace in the night.
The quiet storm, a cherished friend,
In turmoil, grace will mend.

Fragments Lost in Breath

Words unspoken weave the night,
Fragments lost, yet shining bright.
In the hush, a tale unfolds,
Whispered dreams, the heart upholds.

Moments caught in fleeting time,
Echoes fade, but still they chime.
Breathless sighs beneath the stars,
Silent songs and ancient scars.

Capturing the softest gleam,
Memory's dance, a fragile dream.
Time slips through, like grains of sand,
Tales forgotten, all unplanned.

Yet in stillness, hope remains,
Fragments weave both joy and pains.
In the quiet, beauty's breath,
Lives on still, beyond the death.

Embraced by the Unvoiced

In the shadows, silence reigns,
Embraced tightly, hidden strains.
Voices murmur in the dark,
Whispers soft, where dreams embark.

Touched by love, yet unheard,
Every glance, a heartfelt word.
Bond unbroken, though unseen,
In the stillness, souls convene.

Through the veil of silence deep,
Promises made that others keep.
In the night, hearts intertwine,
Captured in a love divine.

Amidst the hush, a spark ignites,
Unvoiced longings, hidden sights.
Together still, despite the night,
In silence, love remains alight.

The Dark Corners of Desire

In shadows deep, where whispers creep,
A longing breathes, in silence steep.
Dreams entwined, like vines that climb,
In secret spaces, lost to time.

Fingers trace, on skin's soft glow,
Hints of passion, buried low.
Each sigh shared, a fleeting chance,
In dark corners, lost in trance.

Moments stolen, a fleeting spark,
Fueling embers, igniting dark.
In depths of night, our spirits soar,
Desires clash, yearning for more.

Winds of fate, they softly blow,
Guiding hearts, where secrets flow.
In shadows cast, we drift and sway,
The dark corners, where dreams play.

Hidden Notes in the Symphony of Life

A melody plays, soft and sweet,
In every heartbeat, a tapping beat.
Notes unwritten, yearn to bloom,
In the silence, a hidden tune.

Laughter sparkles like champagne,
Moments drift like gentle rain.
Harmony croons through the night,
Whispers dance in soft moonlight.

Echoes of joy, bittersweet pangs,
Life's symphony, in subtle tangs.
Notes of love, in shadows cling,
In every heart, they rise and sing.

Together we weave a tapestry fine,
Hidden notes, in rhythm align.
With each breath, we paint the air,
A symphony rich, beyond compare.

Distant Drums of the Unexpressed

In quiet moments, thumping low,
Unheard rhythms begin to flow.
A drumbeat stirs, a heart in flight,
Echoing softly through the night.

Words unspoken, trapped in the chest,
Drums of longing, a silent quest.
Shadows move, creatures of dusk,
In the silence, a vibrant husk.

Rumbling thoughts, a tempest inside,
Hidden meanings our souls confide.
Each pulse drumming a tale untold,
In distant echoes, feelings unfold.

The night is alive with the sacred sound,
In the stillness, we gather round.
Distant drums summon us near,
Unexpressed truths become so clear.

A Tale Told in Silence

In muted gazes, stories unfold,
A tale of whispers, both brave and bold.
Eyes that shimmer, hearts that yearn,
In silence, truths begin to burn.

Softened breath speaks louder than words,
In quietude, the spirit stirs.
Unspoken love dances in air,
Between the lines, we find our share.

Echoes linger, shadows entwine,
A sacred space where we align.
With every pause, a heartbeat waits,
In silence shared, we unveil fates.

The dance of silence, a cherished glance,
In every moment, a fleeting chance.
Through soft embraces, stories revive,
A tale told in silence, we truly thrive.

The Heart's Unheard Plea

In the silence where dreams reside,
Whispers echo, a love denied.
A pulse beats softly in the night,
Yearning for warmth, seeking light.

Beneath the surface, feelings glare,
Hidden glances, longing stares.
The heart calls out, a silent shout,
While the world spins, wrapped in doubt.

Each tear falls like a stolen grace,
Carving trails on a hopeful face.
Yet courage blooms in tender hearts,
Though fear may tear, love never parts.

In shadows cast, the truth will stay,
A melody for souls to play.
When silence fades and voices blend,
The heart's plea finds its voice again.

The Lullaby of What Lies Beneath

Moonlight dances on the deep,
Secrets hidden, tide so steep.
Beneath the waves, whispers flow,
A lullaby of ebb and glow.

Stars glimmer in the velvet night,
Echoes of dreams that take to flight.
The ocean cradles, soft and kind,
Carrying tales, lost to time.

In depths where shadows softly play,
Hopes submerged, drifting away.
Yet in the dark, a spark ignites,
Illuminating forgotten sights.

Awake the stillness, let it sing,
The calm beneath, a soothing wing.
For every wave that crashes loud,
There lies a peace, serene and proud.

Chasing Shadows of Thought

In the corners where echoes dwell,
Thoughts take flight, casting a spell.
Chasing shadows that stretch and bend,
Fleeting moments that twist and blend.

Fingers reach for what slips away,
Each idea like night turning day.
A dance of minds, elusive and bold,
Stories whispered, yet untold.

In the stillness, sparks ignite,
Illuminating the fragile night.
Each shadow holds a truth so bright,
Waiting patiently to take flight.

Yet in the chase, we find our peace,
In shadows danced, our worries cease.
For in the mind's vast, open space,
Chasing shadows brings thoughts to grace.

Illusions of Liberated Silence

In whispers soft, a truth unfolds,
Silence holds more than it beholds.
A dance of thoughts, unspoken dreams,
Where every pause bursts at the seams.

Threads of quiet weave the night,
Crafting tales in muted light.
The heartbeat echoes, steady and clear,
In stillness found, we draw near.

Yet in the shadows, laughter lies,
A symphony beneath the skies.
Illusions flicker, brightly they gleam,
Awakening the quiet dream.

Embrace the hush, let it fully bloom,
In the heart of silence, dispel all gloom.
For in that space, the soul can fly,
In liberated silence, we learn to lie.

Nuances Lost in the Silence

In shadows where whispers fade,
Quiet echoes softly played.
The breath of night holds a sigh,
As dreams in twilight silently fly.

Fleeting moments float like dust,
In stillness, we find our trust.
Yet silence speaks in gentle tones,
A language that dwells in the bones.

Lost passages, time's great thief,
Veils the heart in unspoken grief.
Each thought, a leaf upon the stream,
Drifting softly, a fading dream.

And in this hush, we come to see,
The beauty found in mystery.
Nuances dance in the quiet night,
Capturing shadows, lost from sight.

Lingering Thoughts of What's Left Behind

In the attic of memory's keep,
Dusty dreams that never sleep.
Echoes hum of laughter shared,
In every corner, a love declared.

Fragments scattered, time's embrace,
Each a ghost, a fleeting trace.
We wander through the fractured light,
Seeking warmth in fading sight.

What was once a vibrant glow,
Now whispers soft, a tender woe.
Yet even shadows cast their song,
In the loss, we still belong.

Lingering truths shaped in the past,
Captured in moments that forever last.
We hold on to what time can't sever,
In our hearts, they live forever.

The Space Between Heartbeats

In the quiet, time slips through,
A pause where thoughts form anew.
The heartbeat, a rhythm, soft and low,
The silence cradles the whispers that flow.

Between the beats, a fleeting grace,
A moment held in a sacred space.
Life's melody finds its rest,
As we ponder what matters best.

In this breath, the universe sighs,
A dance of stars in velvet skies.
Each heartbeat a promise to feel,
The depth of love, the weight of the real.

The pauses carve paths unseen,
Between what is and what might have been.
In stillness, we find our way,
The space between leads us to stay.

Secrets Wrapped in Stillness

In the silence, whispers dwell,
Secrets wrapped in a solemn shell.
Beneath the calm, a storm may brew,
Hidden truths, only for the few.

Each gaze, a story yet untold,
In quiet moments, hearts unfold.
The stillness holds what words can't say,
A tapestry woven in shades of gray.

Time's gentle hand cradles the night,
As shadows dance in soft moonlight.
Beneath the surface, mysteries lie,
Waiting to bloom, to soar, to fly.

Let the silence wrap you tight,
A cocoon of thoughts, out of sight.
In secrets sung to the stars above,
We find the stillness, we find the love.

Tides of the Unsayable

Whispers ride the ocean's breath,
Silent waves hold tales of depth.
Secrets flow like rivers wide,
Beneath the surface, truths abide.

Moonlight dances on the sea,
In shadows, thoughts roam wild and free.
Yearning hearts chase fleeting dreams,
Lost in the current, or so it seems.

In the twilight's gentle gaze,
Unspoken words weave through the haze.
Caught between what's said and felt,
In every silence, stories melt.

When night enfolds the restless shore,
The unsayable longs for more.
Tides retreat, then rise again,
Holding hopes where silence reigns.

Hushed Confessions

In quiet corners, secrets lie,
Soft sighs echo, like a cry.
Veiled intentions, hidden sighs,
Lost in whispers, love denies.

A glance exchanged, a fleeting touch,
Words unspoken carry much.
In every heartbeat, a tale untold,
In muted colors, passions unfold.

Underneath the starry night,
Hushed confessions steal the light.
Promises linger on the breeze,
In the stillness, hearts appease.

With every dusk, dreams intertwine,
In silence shared, souls align.
A language forged in tender grace,
In hushed confessions, love finds its place.

The Forgotten Cadence of Hope

Fading echoes of what once was,
Hope dances on the edge because.
Quietly, it whispers low,
In caverns where lost dreams flow.

A heartbeat lost in endless time,
Cadence lingers on the climb.
Unyielding spirit, though forlorn,
In shattered pieces, hope is born.

Through trials faced, the soul grows strong,
In every right, there's a wrong.
Resilience hums an ancient tune,
A melody beneath the moon.

So gather the fragments, piece by piece,
Let the music flow and cease.
For in the silence, hope will bend,
The forgotten cadence starts to mend.

Trails of Unexpressed Sentiments

In shadows cast by softest light,
Unexpressed feelings take to flight.
Paths obscure, yet hearts know well,
Where love resides and sorrows dwell.

Each glance a story, every smile,
A journey walked in hidden style.
Words like petals drift away,
On trails of sentiment, they lay.

In the stillness, absence sings,
Rich are the thoughts that silence brings.
Beneath the surface, feelings bloom,
In quiet corners, love finds room.

Though unvoiced, they linger near,
In trails of hope, we persevere.
For every heart that longs to share,
In silence, connections lead us there.

Milton Keynes UK
Ingram Content Group UK Ltd.
UKHW050901161124
451129UK00027B/107

9 789916 906224